How to Start a Business

Developing Products and Selling Them Online

Entrepreneur Series

John Davidson

Mendon Cottage Books

Mendon Cottage Books

JD-Biz Publishing

Disclaimer

Read before you begin. These business ideas or plans are intended as a guide only! Read these instructions completely through once and understand what is required.

Our books are available at

1. Amazon.com

2. Barnes and Noble

3. Itunes

4. Kobo ,

5. Smashwords

6. Google Play Books

Table of Contents

Introduction

The world of eCommerce is grabbing more and more cyberspace, at lightning speed, than ever before. Online businesses are growing in big leaps and bounds. Selling online is increasingly becoming less of an option and more of a mandatory survival requirement. Online business empires are being created even by those who never thought of making a business worth a few hundred dollars. Looking at Forbes list of the top 10 richest people on this planet, you will realize that more than half of them are techpreneurs who have invested in the world of electronic technologies such as those presented by the marvels of the internet.

These days, you can hardly make your global presence be felt without the aid of the internet. Are you wondering how and where to start doing your business on the internet? This book is just the right key to opening that door to the limitless world of internet business. Don't dwarf yourself to extinction. Grab this opportunity now! Welcome.

We are right here for you. We see you and even before you dare knock, we've already laid out the red carpet for you. This book is a whole world of internet knowledge in itself. From this book, unlimited space awaits you to fill it with your adventurous entrepreneurial prowess. Territories await you in cyberspace for you to conquer and you will be king if you dare make that first move.

Once again, WELCOME!

How to Develop New Products

Figure 2a Developing New Products

Developing products to sell online is no different from the usual process of developing offline products. However, it is the medium of selling them and the target market that makes a huge difference.

The product you develop must be in such a medium that it can be sold online. You can have digital products and non-digital products. Digital products, especially those that are non-tangible, are easy to sell online. Someone just needs to press the download button, pay up, and get the product. On the other hand, non-digital products, especially those that are tangible, would require an extra mode of delivery since the physical product must be delivered through physical means.

Figure 2b Amazon

Online stores such as Amazon and eBay have provisions for selling both tangible and non-tangible products. Amazon is specifically an important site to sell your physical products. You not only sell digital products, but also any tangible products such as clothing, footwear, household electronics, upholstery, jewelry, books, etc.

Amazon is an online store that is visited by millions of customers each day. It is a highly reputable brand that has customer trust. The biggest advantage of Amazon, over other stores, is the Amazon's FBA (Fulfillment By Amazon). Amazon's FBA is a facility that allows you to deliver your products to various physical stores available around the globe. Amazon will take care of everything ranging from branding, packaging, marketing, distributing, selling, and processing of financial transactions, on your behalf. Once you develop your product and deliver to Amazon's FBA center, everything is fulfilled! You can go on vacation, tour the world, or just take time off, and your account will continue make sales and you can withdraw your profits anywhere across the world.

Therefore, having such a facility right in your mind, while developing your product, could save you from a lot of stress and anxiety. They charge for the service, but it is a great way to test the market and get your sales going.

Whichever product you are developing, please know that digital accompaniments are inevitable! These digital accompaniments could be a product description video or eBook, Company description video or eBook, digital advertisement, software snippets, etc. You can never reap maximum benefits from your online business without digital accompaniments. What more? These accompaniments could be sellable products on their own! Thus, it is important to know how to create and market digital products. This is the reason why this book lays special emphasis on digital products.

Let's take an example of the author of this book who earns from holding training workshops and seminars. This is an intangible service, yet, he would need his training services to reach the widest market possible. How would he do it? That's the essence of this book.

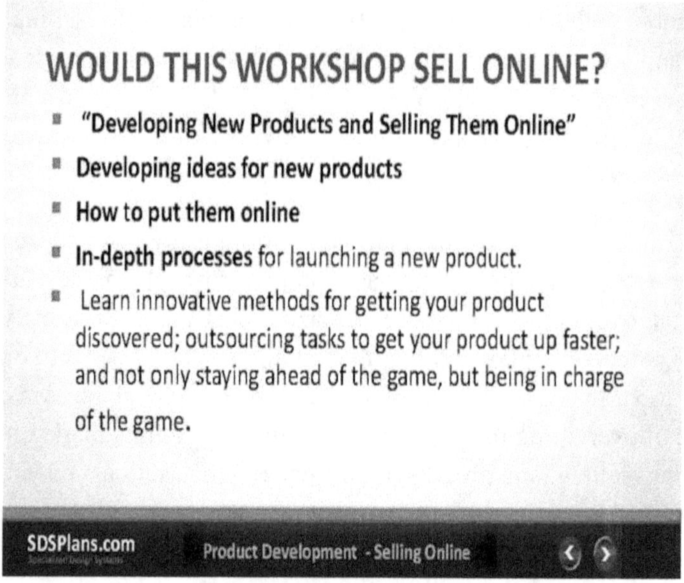

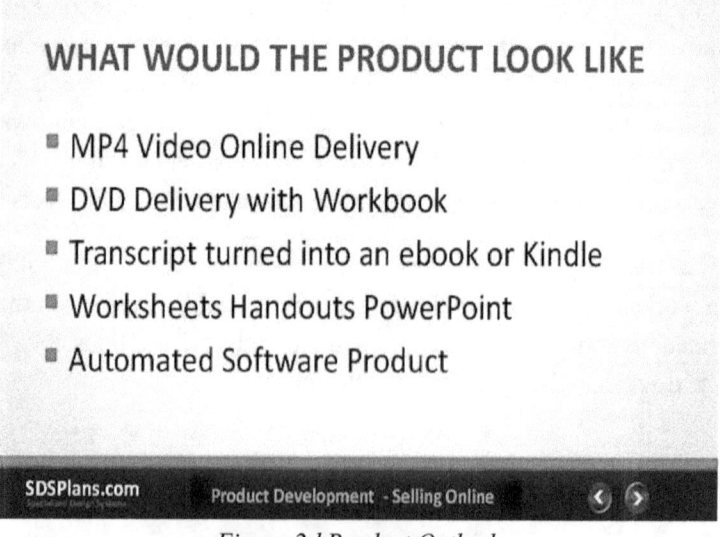

WOULD THIS WORKSHOP SELL ONLINE?

- "Developing New Products and Selling Them Online"
- Developing ideas for new products
- How to put them online
- In-depth processes for launching a new product.
- Learn innovative methods for getting your product discovered; outsourcing tasks to get your product up faster; and not only staying ahead of the game, but being in charge of the game.

SDSPlans.com   Product Development - Selling Online

Figure 2c. Workshop

Fig.2c depicts some of the considerations one would make in selling a training workshop online. Yes, if you are a workshop trainer, you do not just end at the workshop door. You do not need to be just content with the workshop attendance fee, so look further down the horizon! Tap more income from the billions of people across the globe who are online each and every day.

WHAT WOULD THE PRODUCT LOOK LIKE

- MP4 Video Online Delivery
- DVD Delivery with Workbook
- Transcript turned into an ebook or Kindle
- Worksheets Handouts PowerPoint
- Automated Software Product

SDSPlans.com   Product Development - Selling Online

Figure 2d Product Outlook

Now that you have decided that you need to sell your product online, what would your product look like? Take the workshop as an example, as depicted by Fig.2d. There are various forms by which you can package your workshop product; MP4 Video for online delivery, DVD for physical delivery, transcribe your video into an eBook, transcribe your video into slide presentation, etc. Lastly, you can combine all the listed forms and transform them into automated software for downloads.

MP4 Video for Online Delivery

How do you create an MP4 video for online delivery? There are various ways by which you can create an MP4 video for online delivery. The most common of them all is to do video shooting of your event such as a workshop. Once video shooting is done, then you can use MP4 Video converters which are available online for free.

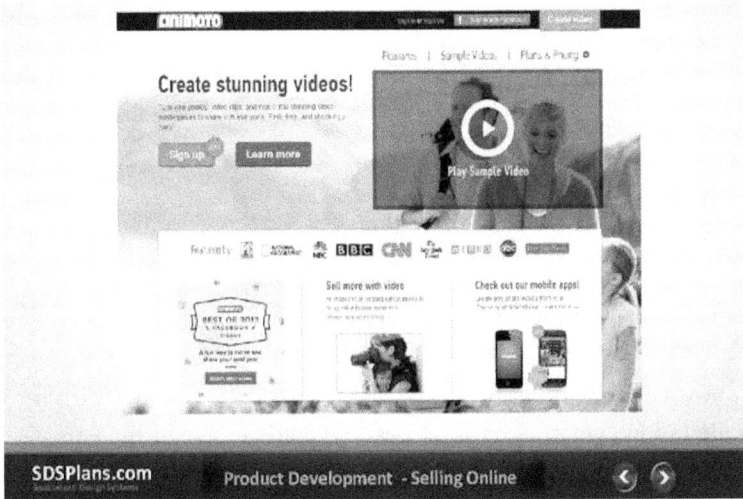

Figure 2e Animoto

The other way to create MP4 Video is to create a PowerPoint slideshow. Once you've created these slideshows, you upload them onto Animoto and they will be converted into videos. Animoto is a specialized online slides-to-videos converter program. Fig.2e shows Animoto website where slideshows can be converted into videos.

DVDs

DVDs are a common way of selling digital products. You can burn your MP4 Video onto a DVD and sell it online on popular eStores such as Amazon, eBay, and others.

Fig. 2f TrepStar DVD making and publishing

There are various ways by which you can have DVD products. Either you can create the DVD yourself or you can take advantage of the various online facilities available to do this for you, at a small fee.

TrepStar is such a nice concept that saves you from the hassles of raising capital to make economic bundles of DVDs and CDS, which range from 200 DVDs/CDs or over at a time. At TrepStar you only need to create content for one CD or DVD, have a logo for the cover page, and upload the content plus the logo. Everything else will be done for you, right from designing the cover to burning on-demand CDs and DVDs, marketing them, selling them, and handling all financial transactions on your behalf. You only need to check your account status and withdraw the rewards of your creativity – All these at only $5 per DVD or CD! TrepStar is the best way to go if you don't want to commit a lot of money for a product you are not sure would pay up for the cost and reward you with handsome profits.

Kunaki is another place to create your DVDs and CDs. The good thing about Kunaki, unlike TrepStar, is that it provides free barcodes. A barcode is mandatory if you would like to sell your products on major eStores such as Amazon. This would save you the cost and time of developing the barcode and make it easy for you to sell your DVDs and CDs on multiple online stores.

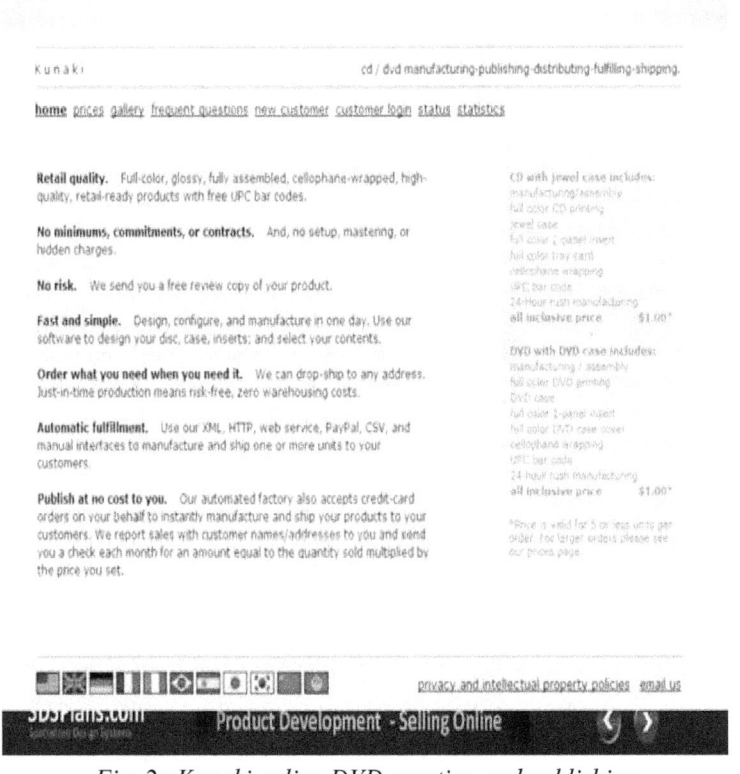

Fig. 2g Kunaki online DVD creation and publishing

EBooks

EBooks are fast becoming the best and most loved way to have book presentation. Once you have created your video, you can easily transcribe it into an eBook. You don't need to worry about the effort and time since there are various ghostwriters online whom you can outsource this work to be done on your behalf. Check on 'How to outsource common tasks' in our table of contents for details.

Fig 2h Bookpatch on demand printing and publishing

The good thing is that you don't need to be an expert in creating various forms of eBooks. You need first to create your eBook in MS Word format. Once your eBook is in Word format, you can convert it to any format needed for an online ebook or printed book!

Fig.2h shows an excerpt from the Book Patch website. BookPatch is an on-demand self-publishing site, whereby you can upload your Word formatted eBook and it is automatically converted into an online eBook format. The advantage of BookPatch is that the book can be sold as an eBook or be printed as hardcopy. Unlike ordinary hardcopy printing, this is on-demand printing where you need not commit huge printing costs incurred as a result of printing in bulky volumes, so as to make economic sense. On-demand printing makes better economic sense, since a single or multiple copies can be printed by the customer as he or she demands.

Other eBook formats include the Kindle format for Amazon, Nooks format for Barnes and Noble, ePub, Mobi, and others. Kindle eBook format is the most popular, and the good thing is that you can easily upload your Word eBook with minor modifications, as per Amazon requirement, to allow it to be converted to Kindle eBook.

Slides

A slideshow is one of the easiest and most attractive ways of presenting your content; be it an eBook, product demo, product description, user instructions manual, events gallery, and many other types of content that you would like to show.

Slideshows have traditionally been confined to desktop publishing, mainly by the use of PowerPoint. However, with business going online, a need for online slideshow presentation became inevitable. SlideShare, as depicted by Fig.2i, shows an online slide presentation.

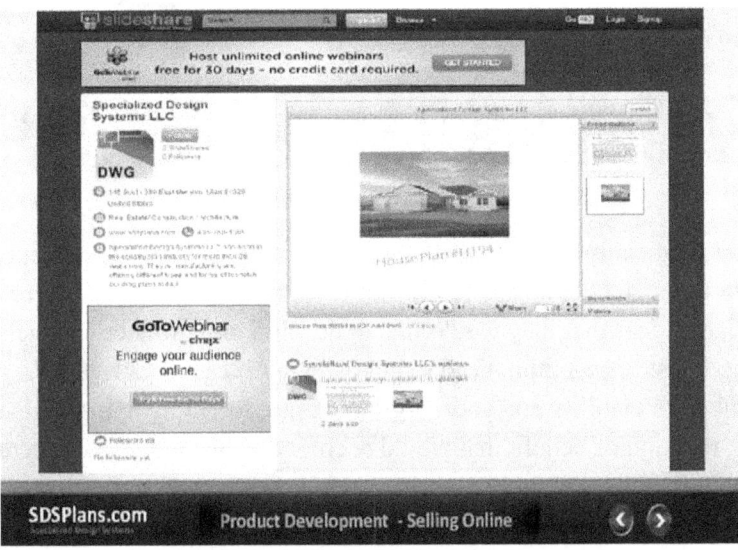

Figure 2i presentation by SlideShare

Once you have created your PowerPoint presentation, you only need to upload it onto SlideShare, follow basic instructions, and all else will be done automatically.

How to Get Funding for your Product Development and Marketing

Fig 2j Raising money thorugh Indiegogo

Are you financially hard-hit so that you cannot develop your product? Kickstarter is there to kickstart your idea. Kickstarter is a place where those with viable ideas that they would like to develop into products can get a funding boost. You simply need to publish your idea on Kickstarter explaining its viability and your target fund, not forgeting to highlight, of course, the kind of benefit that would accrue to your funders. Another online place to get funds to finance your idea is Indiegogo. Kickstarter is more favourable for artistic ventures while Indiegogo is for general business ideas or products.

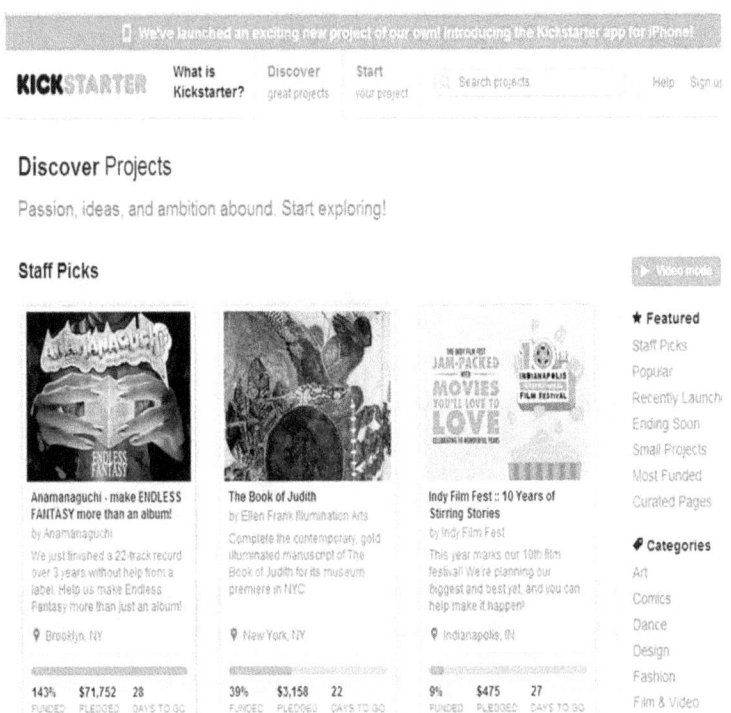

Fig 2k Kickstarter project funding

How to Find a Market for Your Products

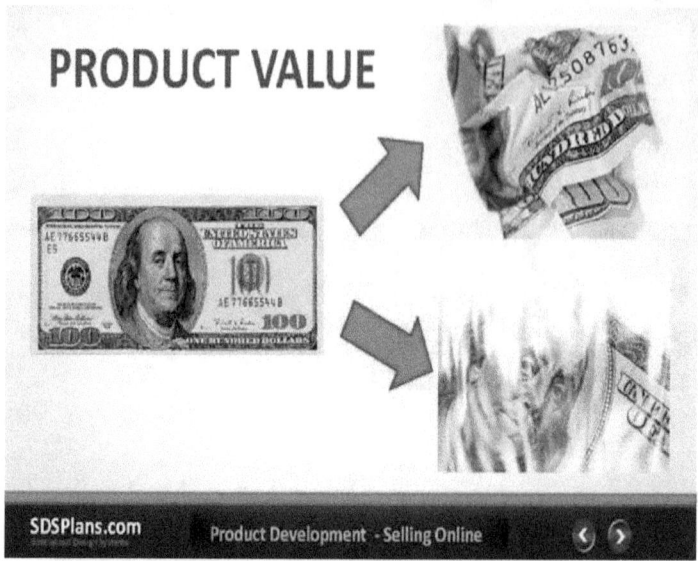

Fig. 3 Product must be in right form to be valuble

The product that you intend to sell must have value to your prospective customers. To have this value, the product must have utility – that is, the ability to satisfy customers' wants. The product must have the utility of time, utility of place, and utility of form. Utility of time simply means that the product must be delivered at the right time. Utility of place means that the product must be delivered at the right place. Utility of form means that the product must be delivered in the right form.

To ensure that your product has value, you must conduct market research. The greatest mistake people make is creating a product thinking that it is such a great product that people will be falling over to buy it. You've got to start with market research first in order to identify customers' wants, so that you can tailor and package your product in such a manner that increases its value to your target customers.

As depicted by fig.4 there are several critical steps that you must follow in ensuring that your product becomes a product of great value to your target customers, especially when you intend to sell your product online.

FINDING A HOT MARKET

- • It contains a large number of people
- • These people are irrationally passionate
- • They have disposable income
- • They have their own jargon
- • They have their own magazines
- • They may hold their own conferences and events
- • They have their own celebrities

Fig. 4 Finding a Hot Market

Finding a hot market

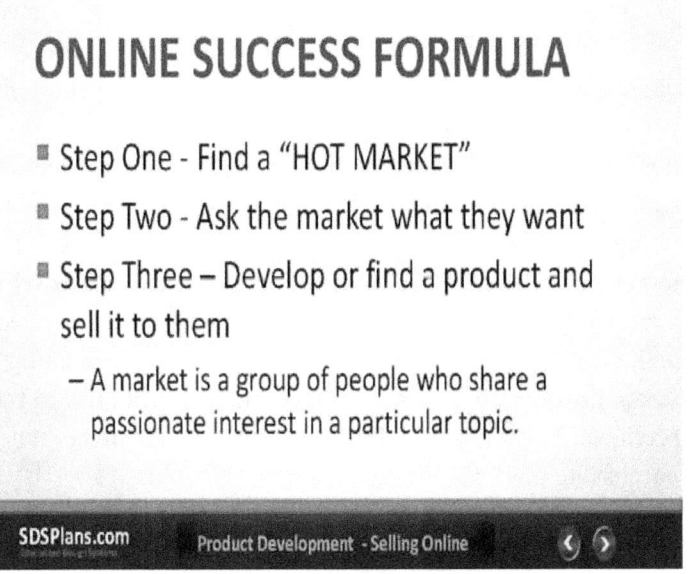

ONLINE SUCCESS FORMULA

- Step One - Find a "HOT MARKET"
- Step Two - Ask the market what they want
- Step Three – Develop or find a product and sell it to them
  - A market is a group of people who share a passionate interest in a particular topic.

Fig 5 Online Success

How do you find a hot market? Finding a hot market requires a combination of skills, experience, and intuition. It is not a straight walk in the park. Nonetheless, there are several tips that can guide you on the way to finding that hot market for your product.

As depicted by fig.5, the top 7 tips for finding a hot market are;

1. **It contains a large number of people**. The bigger the volume of sales the bigger the profits, therefore, you need to find a market with a large number of people to make those huge profits you are wanting.

2. **These people are irrationally passionate**. Having a market characterized by irrationally passionate people is like discovering a shallow goldmine characterized by almost pure gold deposits. You simply need little effort to get that high value. Highly rational people are hardly passionate and buy things because they need them and not because they want them. On the other hand, highly irrational people are extremely passionate; they do buy things because it appeals to their wants and not necessarily their needs.

3. **They have disposable income**. To an Accountant, disposable income refers to that income that you are left with after meeting all the tax obligations and other mandatory deductions from your payroll or gross income. However, to a marketer, disposable income is what is freely available after meeting mandatory expenses that are not just tax and other payroll deductions. It excludes deductions such as rent, school fees, utility expenses, and other mandatory living expenses, so that what is left as disposable income is that money that you can actually 'gamble' with. Yes, this is what can be irrationally spent! One great mistake that many businesspeople make is to target just a large population without evaluating whether or not the respective population has purchasing power to buy the products. The higher the disposable income, the higher the purchasing power.

4. **They have their own jargon**. Yes, people of the same class find a common language to express their common values. If your target market comprises of people who have met the first three criteria and yet they do have their own jargon, then, you've struck a goldmine. Communication is the secret code that helps you to influence your customers' psychology. Once you've mastered their jargon, you've discovered the secret code not only to learn their tastes and

preferences, but also to re-program their mindset to value and appreciate your products.

5. **They have their own magazines**. Do you know the role magazines play in marketing? Magazines are not only a source of advertisement space, but also a great way to learn consumers' lifestyles. If a certain magazine is a hit in a certain market, then, it is a magazine that represents a lifestyle that market has or aspires to have.

6. **They may hold their own conferences and events**. This is another place to learn not only the tastes and preferences of your potential customers, but also the place to learn their lifestyle and behavioral pattern. Attending and participating in such conferences and events is the surest way to learn the secrets of how you need to package your products to suit your potential customers.

7. **They have their own celebrities**. Just like magazines, conferences, and events, celebrities are a pointer to the lifestyle, tastes, and preferences of a particular market segment. Nonetheless, it is also a manifestation of the behavioral patterns of customers within that market segment. By observing celebrities and comparing them with other markets, you would easily understand what interests your potential customers and what turns them off. This would go a long way in helping you package your product in a way that presses that 'passionate irrational button'.

Ask the market what they want

How do you ask the market what they want?

Yes, before you develop a product for a certain target market you need to understand what that particular market is looking for. The challenge is - how do you go about it? There are various ways by which you can inquire and get information of a certain target market and first and foremost, is by reading the market. You can read a particular market by observing its trend, lifestyle, tastes, and preferences from sources such as TVs, Magazines, Newspapers, Blogs, and even social media such as Facebook. Secondly, you can choose to do market survey. Market survey can easily be done online by use of online questionnaires right on your site or social media. Making use of online survey tools such as survey monkey or if you can afford it, engaging a market research company to perform market research on your behalf, is a great idea.

Develop or find a product and sell it to them

You can choose to either develop a product for your target market or simply find an existing product to sell to the target market.

Some people feel that finding an existing product to sell is not such a great idea. However, great ideas are not the ones that sell or bring success. What brings product success in the market is the execution. Therefore, if you can find an existing product to sell, then devise an appropriate execution strategy that is much better than the existing strategies, and you will succeed.

Nonetheless, should you not find a suitable existing product to sell, you would need to develop one. However, you need not necessarily labor so much to re-invent the wheel. Simply make a better wheel. What this means is that it is safer and less risky to redesign and repackage an existing product than to develop a completely new novel idea that you are not sure of how customers would respond to it.

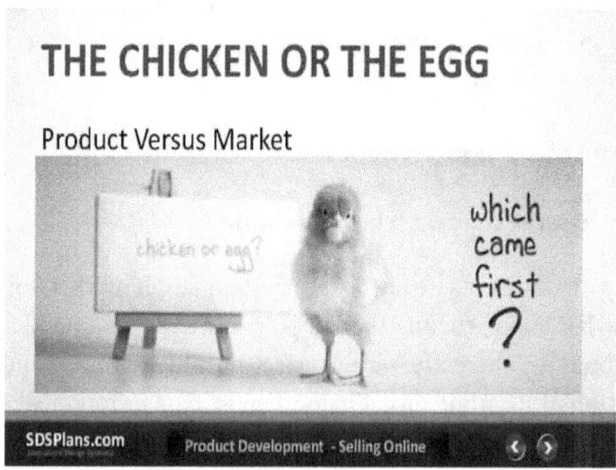

Fig 6 Product VS Market

Product-vs-market what comes first? This is a question that is clearly depicted by fig.6. Yes, it is a chicken-versus-egg kind of question. Whether a product or a market comes first depends so much on your thought – whether you are a producer-oriented or marketer-oriented person. Would you start with a great idea first, or a great market first? It is a great market that shapes a great idea. Thus, before you develop a great product, there has to a great market for it.

How to Sell Your Products Online

Selling products online is one of those exhilarating experiences. It is fun to do. However, not everyone experiences this fun. To succeed in selling online, you need to heighten your search probe and receptive antenna. Yes, it is an adventure that needs tricky exploratory techniques and probing prowess. You've got to understand how to approach the market! You need not get scared though, it is just one of the easiest adventures to make. Here we simplify it for you.

Fig 7 How to approach online market

Fig.7 depicts the top 5 tips on how to approach online market in order to sell your product;

1. **Look for hungry buyers**. Hungry buyers are those buyers with an insatiable appetite for something else that will satisfy their wants. These are the people who will rush to buy your satisfying product once you launch it.

2. **Look for traffic**. Just as you would like to locate your physical shop at a site with a heavy traffic of people, you naturally desire to place your online product on sites with heavy traffic flow of visitors.

3. **Look for problem questions**. Ask, ask, and ask! You need to find that great problem to solve. The greater the problem, the greater the solution. If you really want your product to be a great product in the

market, then, it must be a product that offers a great solution to the great problem in that market.

4. **Look for people seeking solutions**. Yes, there is one thing to have a problem and it is out rightly a different thing to seek solutions. Not all people who have a problem are seeking solutions to their problem. There are those who have surrendered to the problem and trying to wake them from their self-inflicted surrender is like trying to flog a dead horse. On the other hand, there are those who have a problem that they don't even know that the problem exists! In both cases, you would have to be ready to work harder to convince them that you have a solution. The easiest people to convince are those who know the kind of a problem they have and are actively seeking solutions. These are the people who, once you launch your product, would silently shout 'Eureka!' and would most likely rush in droves to buy your product.

5. **Find an evergreen niche**. A great farmer knows that the best trees to provide shade to him and his cattle during hot and dry season, and yet still provide cover during rainy season, are those trees that are evergreen. Yet, this is the same secret that works so well when it comes to marketing. You need not spend lots of your dollars investing in developing a product that will soon perish or become obsolete. You would rather spend your money, time, and effort developing a product that is evergreen, that is, a product with a long life cycle and would still earn you some revenue irrespective of the economic cycles.

Once you've satisfied the above listed criteria or tips, then you are in for proper selling online. The most important thing, before fully launching your product into the market, is you have to do market testing or test marketing so as to gauge the customer's response before channeling all your energies to aggressive marketing. This would help you determine whether the product, as developed, meets customers wants and expectations or whether you would need to repackage it or develop it further or even withdraw it altogether. It is better to withdraw a non-selling product than incur loses trying to force it through the throats of unwilling buyers.

How to Conduct Market Testing

Have you ever thought of food that you've never eaten before? Would you order large quantities of it? Definitely not! You would most likely just take one or a few bites of it to have a taste before taking more bites and ordering bigger quantities. The same happens to your new product in the market. You wouldn't expect customers to just buy it in huge quantities straight away. Only those daring enough would buy straight away. Those who are not risk takers would wait to hear what others have experienced before making their bets.

Similarly, a market is just like a new kind of food for you. Just as your customers want a taste bite, so would you want to experience that taste bite of the market before going full blown into releasing more products into it.

Fig.8 depicts some of the places where you can start off. These places include KSL, Ebay, Amazon, Etsy, Craiglist, etc.

Fig 8 Market Testing

KSL.com, ebay.com, and craiglist.com are great places to test market whatever you want to sell online. These places have huge traffic flows and therefore your product has the advantage of exposure.

There are other specialized markets online such as etsy, Kunaki, and trepstar. Etsy is suitable for selling artistic homemade handicrafts.

Selling digital products

In case you would like to sell digital products such as books, movies, and music, then you do have an upper hand for many more places. Places such as Kunaki and trepstar are ideal for digital products such as DVDs. Indeed, if you are a starter and you don't have much capital, trepstar is such a wonderful place for you. You just need to create a small logo for your DVD and trepster will create an impressive cover, burn the DVDs, sell them, and handle financial transactions on your behalf at only $5 per piece sold. Kunaki also does the same and provides a bar code for your DVDs. Bar codes are a must in case you would like to sell your products on Amazon.

If you are dealing with eBooks, there are several places for you, including Amazon and Bookpatch. Bookpatch has an extra advantage over Amazon – simplicity. At Bookpatch, you only need to upload your eBook in word document format and everything else will be taken care of. Also, at Bookpatch, your eBook gets listed immediately. The other advantage of Bookpatch over Amazon is that Bookpatch offers on-demand printing for hard copies, while Amazon would require you to avail already printed books as hard copies. Amazon does have a new service called Createspace that will allow you to develop on demand printed books and offers them to the Amazon market and other bookstores.

Selling through Affiliates

Is your product such that you do need mass marketing yet you can't afford to employ and manage a huge army of salespeople? Selling through affiliates is the right model for you. Yes, there are online sites that provide a huge salesforce that is affiliated to them and are ready and willing to sell products on your behalf placed on those sites. Such a famous site is Clickbank. Clickbank is such a place to do test marketing since it has thousands of affiliates who will market your products on their sites. This would expose your products to thousands of sites on the internet within an extremely short time. Imagine launching your product and within hours, it is being displayed on thousands of sites! This can't be possible on the normal brick-and-mortar model of selling.

Fig 9 Clickbank affiliate marketing

Other than Clickbank, there are various other affiliate sites online, such as SFI, which operates in a similar fashion, although SFI is more of a multi-level marketing model.

How to Develop Your Products Website

Fig 10 Website components

Your products website is the most important website when it comes to selling your products. As shown in Fig.10, your page should comprise of 5 critical components; squeeze page, sales page, blog, store, Facebook, and YouTube.

A squeeze page is a page as depicted in Fig.11 that serves the purpose of gathering contact details from visitors to your site. These important contact details includes you visitor's name and your visitor's email address.

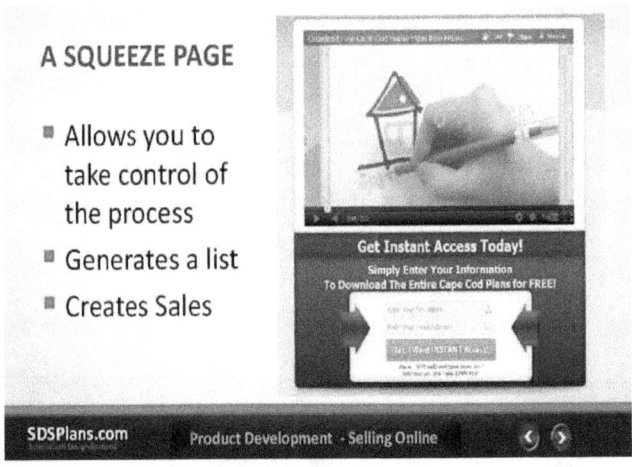

Fig 11 Squeeze Page

A squeeze page allows you to generate an email contact list. An email contact list becomes important when you want to do email marketing. Through email marketing, you can easily promote your products, take customer surveys, and give special offers to target customers.

A sales page is a page where your products are laid out for sale with links to the store. In this page, every product is displayed together with its price. A customer can click on the shopping button displayed as 'Add to shopping cart' in order to add the product to the list of products to purchase. From the shopping cart, there is the 'Check Out' button which a customer clicks after adding all items being bought, so that payments can be made. On the checkout form there are specific details relating to the payment method, e.g. PayPal, Debit/Credit card, etc. Once these details are filled, the customer then clicks on the 'Pay' button to complete the purchase transaction.

A store is basically an extension of the sales page. Once customers click on the 'Buy' or 'Add to shopping cart', they are led to the store where the products can be purchased for download or shipping.

A blog page is a page where extra information is provided that wouldn't otherwise fit in other pages. The blog provides a forum for interaction amongst members and visitors to your site. It also provides an avenue where news about product launches, company policies, product promotions, and other relevant information is found.

Facebook is the most popular social media site. Facebook allows people from all walks of life to interact freely and exchange ideas. With over 1 billion people on Facebook, your website can get huge exposure if you work well on promoting your site on it.

YouTube is one of the top 10 visited sites on the internet today. You can use YouTube to upload video clips that show your product features, demos, and descriptions. You can also use YouTube to showcase your product launch, groundbreaking ideas, and many other important videos.

How to Generate Traffic to Your Products Website

This page must not only be searchable, but must also provide ease of navigation and valued content to the visitors.

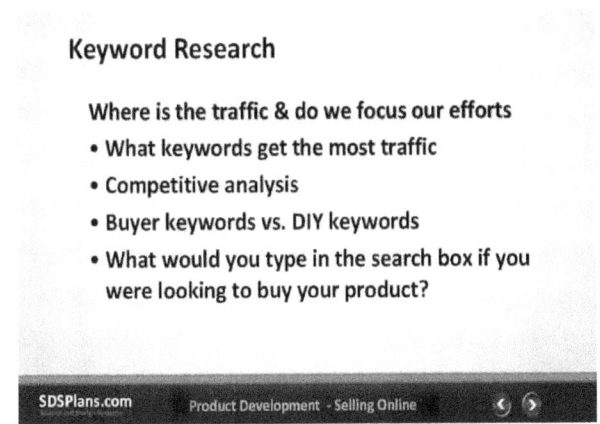
Fig 12 Keyword Research

To make your site searchable, you must use SEO (Search Engine Optimization) techniques. Some of these techniques involve:

1.   Determining the most important keywords

2.   Having an appropriate URL that is rich in Keywords

3.   Ensuring that your content is rich in these keywords

4.   Designing your website so that it's coding and navigation is SEO friendly.

Key words are those special words that searchers use to find a certain item online. For example, if someone is interested in learning how to develop online products, most likely the person would type on the search bar 'developing products online'

On the other hand, those who have already developed these products and are seeking ways to sell them online would most likely type on the search bar 'selling products online'. To have the benefit of both worlds, you would combine the two to have 'developing products and selling them online'.

This combined keyword is known as a long tail keyword since it is a keyword that comprises other keywords in it and certainly makes up a most likely description of what a searcher would be looking for. The keywords within this long tail keyword are 'developing products' and 'selling online'.

How do you find appropriate keywords that most people use to search online? Most search engines, especially Google, have keyword tools that enable you.

Figure 13 Google Adwords

Google Keyword tool, as shown in Fig.13, ranks keywords according to the number of searches per month. The higher the number of searches the more likely your site would be reached if you do use the keyword.

One important secret is to use long tail keywords as part of your product website's url. This will not only improve your sites search ability, but also boosts its ranking.

How to Tap into Popular Traffic Sources

Fig 14 Auxiliary Sites

The fastest way to direct traffic onto your site is to tap into an already existing traffic flow. As shown in Fig.14, there are several places where this traffic flow can be tapped. These places include Facebook, YouTube, eBay, KSL, CraigsList, USfreeads, Etsy, Pinterest, and Amazon.

Facebook is the most popular site on the internet today with over 1 billion followers and still growing. You can tap into Facebook traffic flows by opening up a Facebook page. On your Facebook page, you can put some of your items for sale with links to your products website. You can find creative ways of engaging Facebook visitors to your site by offering freebies, inviting them to like your page, and actively engaging your followers with surprises, such as funny video clips, amazing offers, and new products. Once you get a follower on Facebook to like your page, that liking reflects on that follower's timeline which is visible to that follower's friends.

The best way to expose your page to Facebook fans is to go viral. How do you go viral? Simply create an amazing video or photo and followers of your page will share it with their friends, and these friends will share it with their friends, and friends' friends... ad infinitum – that is viral!

Other than Facebook, YouTube is becoming one of the most followed websites on the internet today. Have a funny video uploaded to your YouTube account, post the links to your website, Facebook page, and request followers to post the same on their website and also, email to their friends. This is another way to go viral.

Do you have an amazing knockdown offer that you auction on eBay? Yes, eBay is one of the most popular auction sites. You can offer some of your products at an amazingly low price, instead of offering them as freebies, and people will be competing to buy them. With a link to your website, this is a good way to tap into eBay traffic flows.

Buying an already existing website or URL

One of the best ways to jumpstart your product sales are to buy a site that has similar products or has a SEO friendly URL. This would ensure that your product would gain instant exposure advantage since the new website or URL is already ranked in the search engines and already has traffic flows.

Fig 14b Places to buy websites

Fig.14b shows some of the places to buy an already existing website. If you can find a website to buy that meets your needs, it is a far better idea than building your own website. However, this depends on the cost-benefit analysis. Should you find that it is expensive to buy the website then you would just have to take the long route of building your own.

At scriptlance you can easily find coders who can develop a new website for you. Flippa is one of the leading places to buy already existing websites for sale.

Fig 14c Flippa

How to Outsource Your Common Tasks

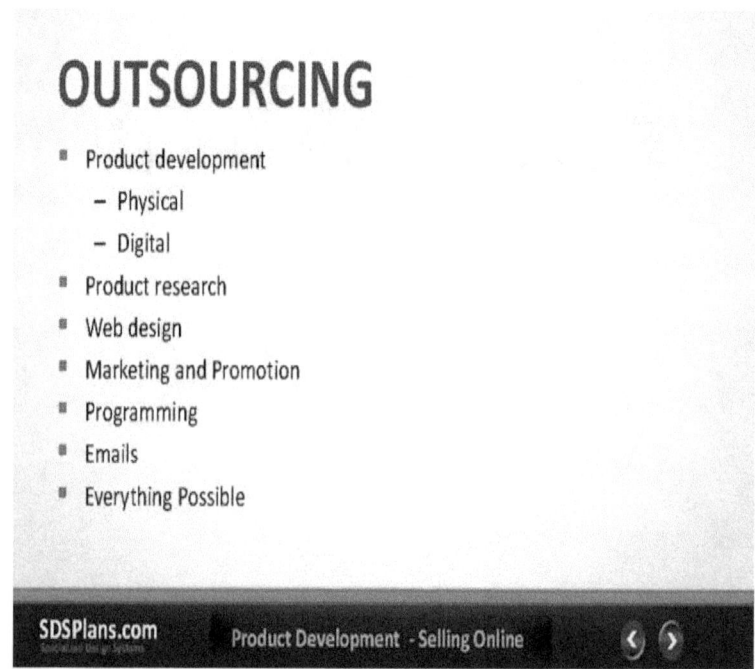

Fig 15 Outsourcing common tasks

Online business requires a lot of varied skills and effort. Therefore, you can hardly do everything on your own. Common skills and tasks that you would require are outlined in Fig.14. Other tasks include optimizing your website so that it can easily be searchable (SEO), monitoring traffic flows, managing your online community, sending sales letters and emails, following up on leads, etc. You cannot afford to do all these alone, yet, it would be too expensive to employ each of these experts to do your tasks on a full time basis.

The best way to handle these tasks is to outsource them – yes, let others do it for you as independent contractors. The advantage of outsourcing to independent contractors is that you not only have a pool of experts, but you also pay for services rendered. You do not need to pay for annual leave, sick leave, personnel medical insurance, and so many other costs associated with hiring permanent staff.

Fig 16 Freelance networks

How do you outsource your common tasks? There are various online sites to find freelancers who can do various tasks on your behalf. Fig.16 shows some of the popular outsourcing available to you.

Amongst these outsourcing sites, Elance and Odesk rank the highest. Each of the two sites operates professionally and provides an opportunity for you to get the best skilled contractors to do your work. However, there is a trade-off between choosing Elance and Odesk. One advantage of Elance over Odesk is that Elance has an escrow account that allows both the contractor and client some degree of certainty. A client can deposit a certain amount of money which is usually an upfront payment or down payment, into an escrow account and this money can only be released to the contractor by the client upon discharge of agreed terms. The client cannot withdraw this money without the consent of the contractor and neither can the contractor access the account. The other advantage of Elance over Odesk is the dispute resolution mechanism. Elance resolves disputes between the client and contractor while odesk does not engage itself in dispute resolution. On the other hand, Odesk has one important advantage, and that is Odesk Team, which is basically software that remotely monitors what a contractor is doing on his computer. Odesk Team is applied for hourly payment contracts and which assures that a contractor bills you according to active hours worked. As Odesk Team captures the screen, keyboard taps, and mouse movements and also has an option for video capture. This ensures that a contractor cannot bill you for hours not worked. The second advantage of Odesk over Elance is that it has no minimum limit of what a contractor can bill you. Elance specifies a minimum limit of about $30 which discourages small tasks to be carried out on it, while Odesk allows as little as $1 and even less for an hourly rate.

How to Market Your Products Website

Online Strategy

THE 3 KEYS TO SUCCESS ONLINE

- **Targeted Traffic:**
  Steady/Ongoing targeted traffic from multiple sources
- **Conversions:** An engaging website that turns visitors into customers
- **Repeat Sales:** A system for getting the 1st, 2nd, 3rd, 4th sale and beyond plus referrals

SDSPlans.com   Product Development - Selling Online

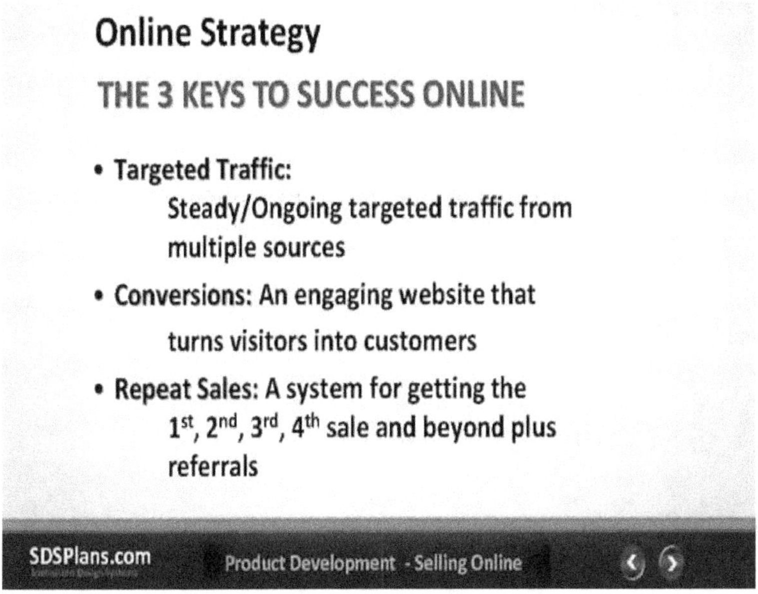

Fig 17 Online strategy

To market your products website, it requires clever strategies. Some of these strategies as outlined in Fig.17 include targeted traffic, conversions, and repeat sales.

Targeted Traffic

Targeted traffic is that traffic that flows from an already defined source. Before you start marketing your products website, you need to do some prior research to know what potential customers are looking for online, in terms of the keywords they use to search for your product and also the kind of sites they visit most.

There are various ways by which you can establish targeted traffic. These include:

SEO Marketing

Online Directories

Auxiliary Sites

SEO Marketing

We briefly looked at SEO under 'How to generate traffic to your products website'. This was basically using the internal mechanisms, that is, optimizing your website for SEO purposes. However, you can also apply external mechanisms, which means using SEO on other websites to drive traffic to your site. This is what is called SEO Marketing.

As depicted by Fig. 18, some of the SEO Marketing tools include Press Releases, Articles, Videos, Slides, and photos.

Fig 18 SEO Marketing

Press Releases

A Press Release is a special statement that is geared towards providing factual information to the public about an organization's status, events, and activities such as an anniversary celebration, product launch, new product features, key staff hiring, key staff promotion, a new technological breakthrough, special offers, etc.

A Press Release is a good way to subtly market your product without being overly loaded with a sales pitch. A Press Release needs to be SEO friendly in order for it to generate traffic.

There are various Press Release sites such as PR Web and Area-Info (shown in Fig.18a) with huge traffic flows that can easily direct traffic to your products website.

Fig 18a Area info PR site

SEO Articles

Articles have of late taken a huge chunk of online marketing. People seem to be fatigued by billions of bombarding advertisements, such that they avoid pop ups by employing pop up blockers and the like. Therefore, a subtle advertisement where a prospective customer is persuaded through an informative yet, professional article, is the best way to go.

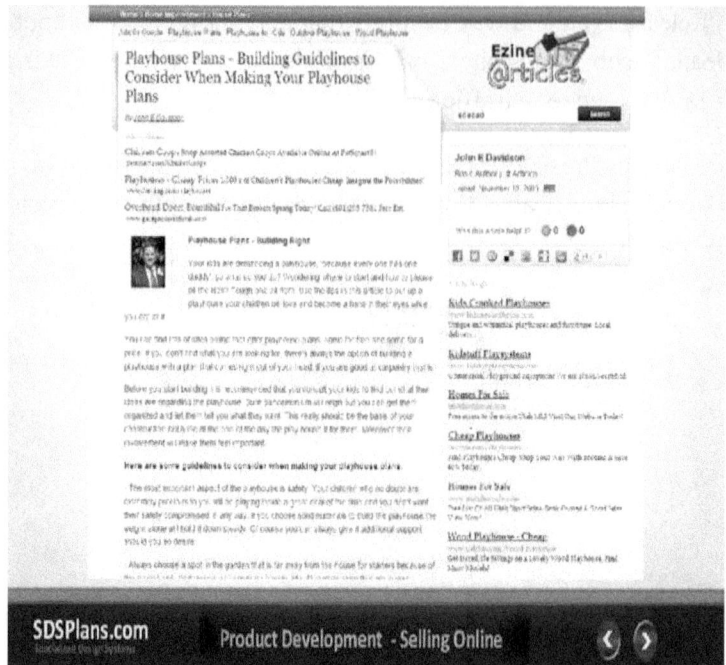

Fig 19 Ezine

A SEO article is different from an ordinary informative article in the sense that it has SEO keywords that attract traffic to it. Once the traffic is attracted to it, it is then deflected back to your products website. For this deflection to succeed, the article must be put in such a persuasive and professional manner that would inspire readers to follow links outlined in it, of which these links leads to various pages or segments of your products page.

You can easily outsource writing of these SEO articles to outsourcing sites such as Odesk, Elance, and Freelancer. You can either post these articles yourself to online article directories or let your contractor easily do it for you.

Some of the common online article directories include ezine articles (shown in Fig.19), linkvana, squidoo lens, ehow, etc.

Videos

They say a picture speaks a thousand words. Well, what about a motion of hundreds to thousands of pictures, accompanied by spoken and written words? Yes, that's video and the a million words it is capable of communicating.

There are billions of text contents to read online. This can bring heavy fatigue on readers. To have an alternative mode of delivery that can relieve this fatigue and drive your point home fast, you need to use the power of video.

Spend a little time, effort, and money to make up a video that describes your product, its features, its usage, and how to get it and you will have tapped a huge market.

19a types of videos to create

Luckily, if you are not a professional in this, you can get a professional contractor, from the plenty of outsourcing sites available, to do a video for you.

Once you have completely done your video, simply create a free YouTube account, and upload it. This has the capability of reaching traffic of over a billion visitors. To enhance this exposure, you can embed the same video on your products' website and attach links to various other auxiliary sites such as Facebook, Twitter, LinkedIn, Pinterest, Stumble Upon, and so many others.

Slides

Do you ever hear talk of PowerPoint online? Yes, there are various sites online such as Slide Share that enables slide presentation. The goodness of slide presentation is that it is a sleek way of presenting content within a limited space.

On sites such as Slide Share (shown in Fig.19a), you only need to upload your content and the content will be converted into a slide. Slide Share is such a site that receives a huge traffic flow, which you can easily redirect to your products website.

Wondering how to do it? You need not worry, because there are plenty of contractors on outsourcing sites who are ready to do it for you at extremely affordable rates.

19a Slide Share

Photos

Photos are a good way to capture attention. A photo easily represents information at a glance. Having a photo that is SEO friendly, which means having a caption and 'alt' (alternative text to photo), that is search engine optimized accompanied by appropriate links, can easily drive traffic to your site.

You not only need to place interesting and professionally done photos on your products site, but you also need to place such photos on sites like Facebook, Pinterest, Flickr, stumble upon, Tumblr, LinkedIn, etc. This would grant your products page maximum exposure.

Online Directories

There are various online directories where you can register your products website and products. You can also post articles on these online directories.

Fig 20 Online Directory

Some of the popular online directories include yellow pages and craigslist. You can also use article directories such as ezine articles, linkvana, squidoo lens, EHow, etc. Other online directories are listed in Fig.20.

Auxiliary Sites

We had previously talked about auxiliary sites such as Facebook, Twitter, YouTube, etc. These sites are good for you to embed links to your products website.

Online stores are also a good way to market your products website. You simply need to take a sample of your products and post them on online stores such as Amazon, eBay, Etsy, KSL, and others with links to your products website. This is so potential customers can not only buy from such sites, but also can click on the product's link which leads them to your website.

Blogs and Forums

Blogs and forums are a good place to market your products website. You would need to check for blogs and forums that focus on products similar to your own or touching on the industry to which your respective products belong to. Give comments on such blogs and forums with links pointing to your product's website.

You can also establish your own blogs as part of either your website or as independent blog or both. This would improve on interactions with both existing and potential customers.

Conversions

However nice your products site is, if it can't convert visitors into customers, repeat customers and referrals, then it is not such an asset. What brings about site conversion? There are several factors that facilitate conversion:

Site Mechanics

Marketing Campaigns

Traffic flows

Site Mechanics

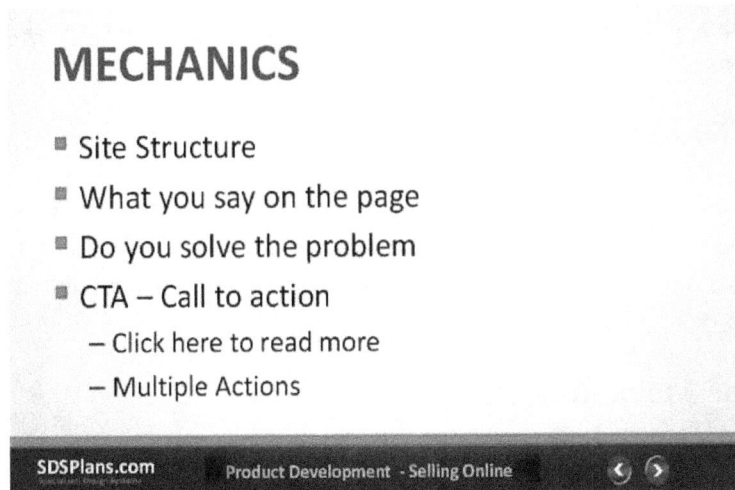

Fig 21 Site Mechanics

Site mechanics refers to how your site is designed, starting from the coding, content display, content language, and content value. Fig.21 shows some of the important consideration in the site mechanics.

Site Structure

Your products site should be structured in such a manner that not only optimizes on search ability, but also optimizes on navigability. The site should be easy to use and easy to navigate from one page to another to and from.

Content value

The content you put on your site should not only describe what you say, but also how you say it. What you say must be such that it is factual. How you say it, concerns it with how you express your language and answers the following questions; is your language easy to understand? Is your language clear and concise? Is your language courteous and respectful? All these add to content value, which would inspire potential customers.

Do you solve the problem?

There is no need to spend your time and effort deriving tons of content that is irrelevant to the potential customers' needs. Your content and the website as a whole must solve the problem that the potential customer is seeking solutions to.

Call To Action – CTA

Have you excited the potential customer enough to press the 'BUY BUTTON'? You must create the need and urgency in the potential customer's psychology so that the customer can feel how inevitable it is to buy the item.

Online Marketing Campaigns

Online marketing campaigns can be carried out through various means that include:

Email Marketing

Adverts

Use of classified ads

Use of social media

Placing your products on online stores

Weekly promotion campaigns

Email Marketing

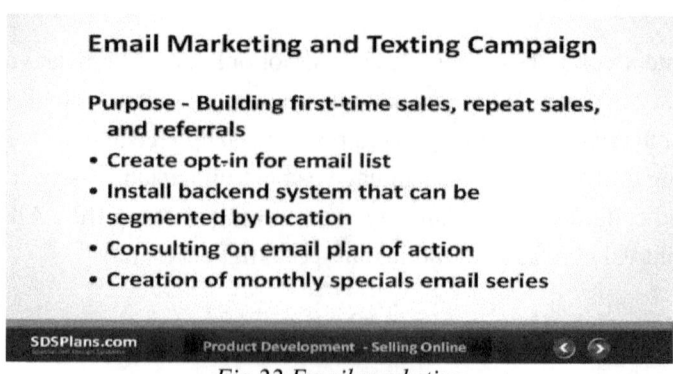

Fig 22 Email marketing

Email is one of the easiest ways to market your products. Once you have emails of customers and potential customers, then it is easy to make sales promotions through their emails.

There are various online facilities that can help you manage your email marketing campaigns. One of these tools is Call Loop.

Fig 23 Call Loop

Fig.23 depicts Call Loop facility. Call Loop helps you to manage your email campaigns by making it easy to create instant and periodic email newsletters and post them automatically to the listed emails. Call Loop also has SMS text facility that helps you send mass SMS automatically to listed mobile phone numbers.

Advertising

Advertising is a popular means of advertising online due to the ease, flexibility, and affordability of online adverts. Online adverts, unlike outdoor or radio and TV adverts, are extremely flexible in terms of budget. You can have adverts for as low as $5 or even free!

Fig 24 Traffic

Fig.24 shows the various types of sources of traffic. Organic traffic is one that arises out of visitors own effort to arrive at your site. Paid traffic is one that is directed to your site through advertisement. This paid traffic can be derived from PPC (Pay Per Click) or PPV (Pay Per View). PPC is a mode of payment whereby you pay per every click on the posted advert. Therefore, the click becomes the recognition that the advert has attained its objective. PPV is a mode of payment whereby you pay per every view of a posted advert irrespective of whether the advert is clicked on or not. PPV is generally cheaper than PPC, but with a lower conversation rate (that is, turning visitors into customers).

Fig 25 DirectCPV

There are various online advertisement companies including Google, Facebook, DirectCPV, Sitescount and Etsy. Each of these advertisement companies has its advantages and disadvantages. Google is so far the most expensive of them all, and its adverts have the widest reach. Facebook has the second widest reach. However, Facebook allows you to make adverts for as low as $5.

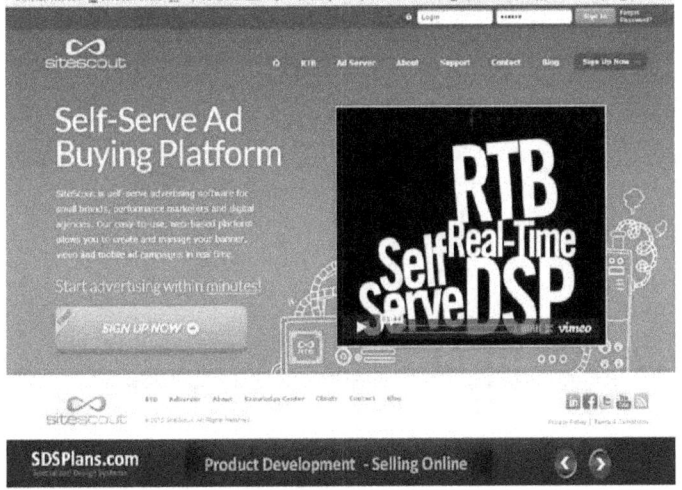

Fig 26 Sitescount

Use of Classified ads

There are various sites that provide space for classified ads either free or at a small fee depending on the type and extend of service that you require.

Some of these classified ads sites include:

KSL

USFreeAds

Fig 27 KSL

KSL.com allows you to post classified ads. KSL is one of the largest classified ads site and has millions of visitors. Placing your ad on KSL can bring a huge traffic to your products site where customers can buy. USFreeAds is another place to put your classified ads. For only $6 per month subscription, you can have plenty of ads on USFreeAds, which will generate lots of traffic to your products site leading to increased sales.

Use of Social Media

Social media has billions of members. The three leading social media sites to place your adverts are:

Facebook

Twitter

Pinterest

Fig 28 Facebook

You can easily open up a Facebook page like the one shown in Fig.28, where you can arrange your products and put links to your site where customers can buy the products. This is the cheapest way of generating traffic from Facebook into your products site.

Fig 29 Twitter

Twitter is another place to put up your adverts. Although twitter is so limited in its usage, such that it mainly allows text, you can create a text with a link and tweet it which works like a massive online 'SMS'. The good thing about twitter is that you can easily integrate it into your own website as shown in in Fig.29 above.

Pinterest is such a wonderful social media where you can display your photos just as you would do with a classified ad. However, unlike classified ads, there is no provision for you to quote prices and put the 'buy' button that would lead to shopping cart. Therefore, you can put photos of your products with links to your respective products page as shown in Fig.30.

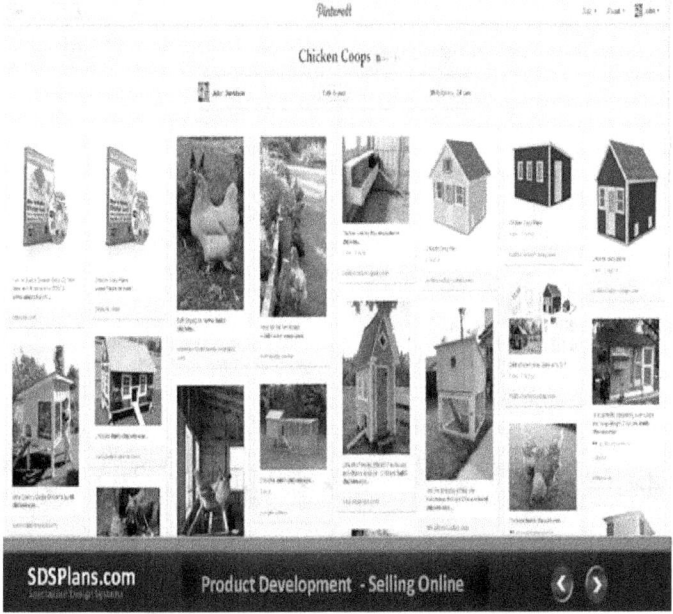

Fig 30 Pinterest

Placing your products on online stores

One other way to market your products is to place them on online stores. There are various major online stores whose suitability depends on your nature of product. The following are some of the major stores online:

Amazon

EBay

etsy

clickbank

Both Amazon and eBay sells virtually every kind of product.

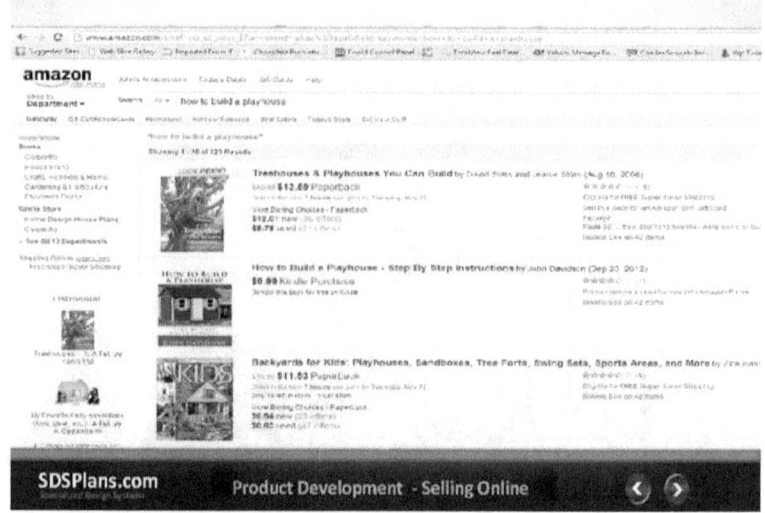

Fig 31 Amazon

Amazon

Amazon is the world's largest online store that deals with virtually every kind of product. Amazon sells millions of items a day and thus has an extremely huge traffic flow. Furthermore, other than being able to sell on Amazon, it also gives you an opportunity to have backlinks to your products page and even provides an opportunity for a free press release about your product.

Ebay

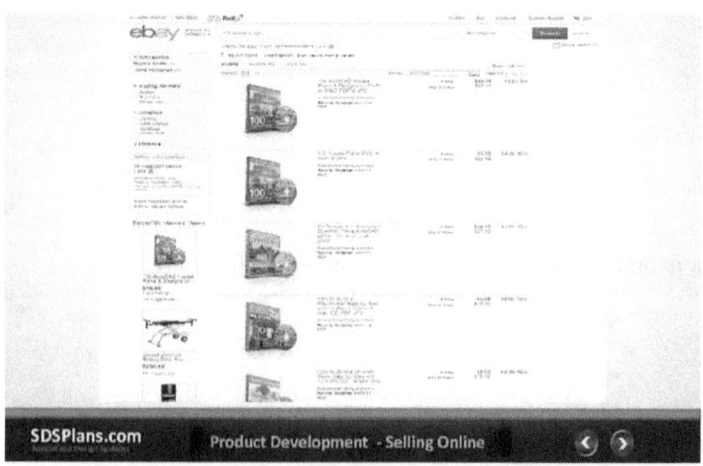

Fig 32 EBay Store

EBay is the leading competitor of Amazon and equally receives huge traffic and has hundreds of thousands of products on its online store. This makes it an important market to place your products for sale and also receive backlinks to your products website.

Clickbank

Clickbank is one of the largest online affiliate sites today. It has hundreds of thousands of affiliates who market products on its site. Other than displaying your products on Clickbank, most affiliates have their own websites which display your products on them. This acts like a free advert for your products. Clickbank is also a good source of backlinks to your products website.

Etsy

Fig 33 Etsy

Etsy is a good site for selling products online. Etsy is ideal for small items, especially handicrafts and household items. At etsy, you only need to pay about $0.2 per item plus about 3% of sales made. The other great advantage of etsy is that you can pay to have your product rank high in addition to having your own shopping cart.

Weekly promotional campaigns

WEEKLY PROMOTION METHOD

- Write a press release or article and submit
- Turn it into a Slide Show and submit
- Turn it into a video and submit
- Post on my Blog, Facebook, Twitter
- Weekly Newsletter or Blog Summery to List
- Bookmark, Ping

SDSPlans.com   Product Development - Selling Online

Fig 34 Schedule of weekly promotions

Marketing, though easy to do, requires a high level of frequency. To maintain and improve your products' online presence, you need to have a weekly promotional campaign as outlined in Fig.34. This weekly promotional campaign would not only ensure that there is increased traffic flow, continued exposure of your products online, but also improved search engine ranking which would further expose your products website to more traffic flow.

Automated promotion

Fig 35 Onlywire and oneload

We have looked at all the outlined methods of promoting your products. However, it is not so easy to promote your website onto dozens of available media, such as video media and social media, on weekly basis without the help of automation.

As indicated by Fig.35, there are two good facilities for automating weekly promotions; OnlyWire and OneLoad.

OnlyWire is a social media automating facility whereby you put up your promotion that you expect to go to social media, and it will automatically post on all your existing social media such as Facebook, Twitter, LinkedIn, etc.

OneLoad is a video sharing automating facility whereby you upload your promotional video on it and it automatically posts the video on all leading Video Channels and sites.

With these two automating facilities, you can save loads of time, effort and money.

Conclusion

Developing products and selling them online has become not only the most effective and efficient way of doing business, but also the ultimate means of reaching billions of potential customers worldwide. Establishing your online presence can be, at times, a cumbersome and expensive endeavor if not well informed and organized. This book provides the much-needed practical information and guidelines that can enable you to maximize benefits out of your product and business endeavor. Yet, the book alone cannot satisfy all the modes of communication that can enable you to have an all-round perspective. You need to attend workshops and seminars such as those conducted by John Davidson or watch his highly educative and inspirational videos. Visiting some of his sites such as http://sdsplans.com would be the best way of understanding how he has managed to be a successful online entrepreneur, and from which source the inspiration to write this book emanates.

About the Author

John Davidson is an online products development guru who has been developing and selling products online since the year 2000. John is an accomplished writer, trainer and highly successful guest speaker conducting various educational seminars pertaining to his pet subject – online business development. As a writer, John has published over 500 books and sold over 500,000 copies of them online.

John is an accomplished Architectural draftsman who has successfully utilized the power of eCommerce to sell thousands of architectural plans worldwide. As an internet business entrepreneur, John runs over 200 websites managed under his company – Specialized Design Systems which comprises of full-time staff and freelancers located across the globe.

As an internet techpreneur, John has developed dozens of mobile apps with over 300,000 downloads so far. Before venturing into business online, John has been drawing homes, barns, and garages since 1984. He has drawn over 500 homes and over 1000 garages and barns thanks to his family drafting business Specialized Design Systems.

On one of his architectural design websites, http://housecabin.com has over 100 full house and cabin plans available for easy download for as low as $1 each. John has been selling affordable digital plans online for over 10 years. Check out more of his plans at http://sdsplans.com which is Specialized Designs Systems LLC plan website.

John's newest project is a series of nonfiction children's books about animals geared towards young readers the website is http://AmazingAnimalBooks.com

This book was developed from a lecture John gave at the Cache Business Resource Centers Business Summit.

Check out some of the other JD-Biz Publishing books
Gardening Series on Amazon

Learn To Draw Series

How to Build and Plan Books

Our books are available at

1. Amazon.com

2. Barnes and Noble

3. Itunes

4. Kobo

5. Smashwords

6. Google Play Books

Publisher

JD-Biz Corp

P O Box 374

Mendon, Utah 84325

http://www.jd-biz.com/

www.ingramcontent.com/pod-product-compliance
Lightning Source LLC
Chambersburg PA
CBHW070932180526
45168CB00003B/1050